# Teacher
## TURNED...

BY
## ARIANNA VERNIER

ISBN 979-8-9873327-1-9

# DEDICATION

To the teachers who just want to know that there are other possibilities out there, this is for you.

To my husband and my babies, the reason I do what I do each and every day. Thank you for always supporting me in my journey. I love you more than words.

# A NOTE TO THE READER:

I wrote this book through the lens of teaching because that is where I have the most experience. However, even if you're not a teacher, you are more than welcome here. I believe that if you've picked up this book, God has asked you to pick it up for a reason.

# CONTENTS

# INTRODUCTION:

## *The Call*

"Commit your way to the Lord. Trust Him and He will act."

Psalms 37:3

"You can't be a stay-at-home mom."

When my husband said this to me shortly after we got married, I was crushed. And while I knew he was right and that we needed my income, it still broke my tired, burnt-out teacher heart.

Growing up, there were two things I always knew. One was that it was my deepest desire to become a mom. The second was that I was really good with kids.

My first job was babysitting the neighborhood children. I worked in a daycare and after-school program for several years and taught camps in the summer. After that experience, it seemed like the next "right" step for me was to go into teaching. I didn't really bother taking the time to explore other options or to really analyze if this was something that would allow me to achieve the goals I had for myself and my future family. Everyone knew me as a teacher, so it was only fitting that I would choose teaching as my career.

Fast-forward to my third year of teaching and my second year of marriage, and I knew that this was not something that I was meant to do long-term. I mean, don't get me wrong, I loved my students, but I knew that all the extra expectations placed on teachers' shoulders would not allow me to become the mom I desired to be. I wanted to be there for all our kids' firsts, pour into them as much as I could, and be present for them. I knew that coming home each day exhausted, stressed, and left with patience the size of a grape would not allow me to be the best mother I could be to my own kids. I also knew that in order to live the life that my husband and I wanted for our family, we couldn't do it on one income. It was incredibly important to us to get out of debt, spend an abundance of time together, and be able to travel freely. I had to figure out how to make this dream of being home with my kids a reality, while still helping my husband provide for our family.

In my third year of teaching, I got pregnant with our daughter. After sitting down and weighing our options, my husband and I decided that I would take a year off from teaching, so I could pour into our new little girl's life. Then at the end of that year, I would go back to the classroom. Little did I know that when I left the school for my year-long maternity leave, it would be the last time I set foot in a classroom as a teacher.

It's funny now looking back and seeing all of God's little nudges toward finding my true purpose in life, but it wasn't so funny then. And once I realized I wasn't going back, I questioned God a lot about what I was really meant to be doing. Going into teaching was what I felt was expected of me and where I felt the most comfortable, and once I quit, it was a challenge to figure out who I was outside of being a teacher. Motherhood was everything I had ever dreamed it would be, but I could also sense that God was calling me to something even bigger. I just didn't know what it was.

This, my friend, is where you come into the story. Maybe you see bits and pieces of yourself in my journey out of the classroom. Maybe like me, you went into teaching because it made the most sense, without taking the time to figure out if that's where you want to be long-term. Or, maybe you really did think your purpose was being a classroom teacher, but the years of stress, lack of support, and constant additions to your plate have made you lose that love for teaching that you once had, and you're trying to figure out what your purpose might be outside of the identity of "teacher."

Sister, if you take away one thing from this book, my hope is that you come to believe that God put you here for a reason. He has a plan and a purpose just for you. Purpose isn't something that can be lost. It's something that is already within you, waiting to be uncovered. You are a Daughter of the King, and He wants you to know what your purpose is. You may not know why you're here or where you're going, but when you look back at your life a few years from now, I pray that God shows you exactly why you've experienced those trials and tribulations.

Throughout the rest of this book, we're going to take a deep dive into uncovering your God-given identity outside of teaching. I'm going to walk you through seven steps to unlocking your purpose and overcoming anything that's holding you back using my PURPOSE framework. (See what I did there?) The process of finding your PURPOSE outside of teaching is as follows:

*P*ray

*U*ncover

*R*edefine

*P*rioritize

*O*vercome

*S*et Goals

*E*valuate

Each chapter will give you practical tools you can implement into your life that will help you figure out why God put you here on this earth. I hope that this book not only gives you the gentle kick-in-the-pants you need, but that it also feels like I'm giving you a warm hug and saying, "Sister, I know how you feel." It's my prayer that by the end of our time together, you will have a clearer understanding of what your purpose is outside of teaching, and that you put this book down feeling on fire for the life God has given you.

Are you ready to unlock your purpose, overcome the obstacles that get in your way, and live the life that God designed just for you? Grab my hand, friend—let's do this together.

## LET ME HELP.

Sister, I want to be with you every step of the way as you work to uncover your purpose outside of teaching. To help you even more, I've put together a free guide, so I can partner with you as you work through this book. I'll share extra resources and even offer some free downloads that will help you dive deeper into the process of uncovering your purpose outside of teaching. You can grab the free guide at teacherturnedvirtualassistant.com/resources.

# CHAPTER 1:

## Pray

"Do not be anxious about anything, but in every situation, by prayer and petition, with thanksgiving, present your requests to God."

Philippians 4:6

When I first quit teaching, I didn't know who I was anymore. I didn't know what my purpose was outside of being a new mom to my sweet baby girl, and I just wanted God to give me a clear roadmap that would show me how to get from where I was to where He wanted me to be. I wanted to know exactly what was coming next, so I could anticipate it and brainstorm exactly how to handle every situation.

*Unfortunately. That's not how God works.*

One important thing to understand about God is that He's not going to give you the entire roadmap at once. If you could see exactly what He has waiting for you, you would most likely say, "You want me to do that?! I don't even know how!" And then you would probably stay where you are, feeling utterly overwhelmed.

*Spoiler alert*—You don't need to know every step of the path God is calling you to take. You just need to take that first step of faith, and allow Him to uncover the next step when He thinks you're ready.

I knew I was meant to do something other than teaching, so I started praying that God would show me exactly what that was. Then, on the day I went into labor, I came across the term "Virtual Assistant" and immediately thought, "God, is this the answer to my prayer?" Later that night, I started having strong contractions, and I knew it was time to go to the hospital. I like to think I'm pretty good at noticing God's winks when He sends them my way, so it wasn't lost on me that He showed me this potential option to work from home with my baby girl on the exact day that I went into labor. Taking that as my sign, I decided to take a step of faith and pursue becoming a Virtual Assistant.

From that point on, I started learning everything I could about the Virtual Assistant world. Every time my daughter was napping or I couldn't fall back asleep after a midnight feed, I was researching how to become a successful Virtual Assistant. Within a few months I had already replaced half of my teaching income while my newborn was napping beside me, and within six months I had replaced my income completely. I was so happy that I was able to help my husband provide financially for our family while still spending my days with her. I thought, *This is it—this is what I'm meant to do for the rest of my life.*

But (isn't there always a "but"?) I started to notice that I still didn't feel complete. I had a lot of success, and many of my teacher friends were starting to ask me how they could become Virtual Assistants as well. I started getting more and more teachers coming my way asking for advice. At first, this made me nervous. I still saw myself as "just a former kindergarten teacher", not someone who was qualified to be giving other teachers career advice. However, I was starting to feel that nudge again, and I knew that God doesn't call the qualified-He qualifies the called. So I prayed that God would clarify my purpose even further.

And He did. After taking some time to pray, I knew that God was asking me to help other moms and teachers achieve their dreams of quitting teaching. He helped me create the Teacher Turned Virtual Assistant Program and the Ditch the Classroom Podcast, so I could serve as many teachers as possible-and the rest is history.

This is quite a summarized version of how I got to where I am today, but one key element that I hope you take away from my story is this: every time I started to feel like I didn't belong where I was, I began praying.

And that brings us to the first P of the PURPOSE framework—*Pray.*

If it weren't for turning to prayer, I would not have learned about the Virtual Assistant world. If it weren't for prayer, I wouldn't have been able to help all the women I have who also wanted to work from home with their babies. If it weren't for prayer, I would probably still be teaching, feeling stuck and unfulfilled.

*Prayer is the way we draw closer to God. and it's through prayer that He can speak to us and show us exactly where He's calling us to go.*

Those God-sized dreams on your heart will probably make you nervous, but they should also excite you. They will make you question, *How is this even going to be possible?* This is a question you can bring to God in prayer, and it's one that He loves to answer. Our Father is a God of miracles, and He can make anything happen. All we need to do is have a little (or a lot of) faith.

Maybe you're wondering, *Okay Arianna, but I'm not really sure how* to *pray effectively.* Or maybe you're thinking, So, *do I just have* to *sit there and pray for hours and every dream I have will come true?* Probably not. But don't worry sister—I'm going to walk you through a few easy ways to start incorporating prayer into your search for purpose.

## 1. PRACTICE GRATITUDE

When was the last time you thanked God for what you have?

I know, I know, you're not happy with where you're at in life, which is why you're reading this book. But humor me for a second. When was the last time you told God thank you?

*Gratitude* is one of the fastest ways to start figuring out exactly where you want to go in life and how you can get there the fastest. The Merriam-Webster Dictionary defines gratitude as "the state of being grateful." Its synonyms are appreciation, appreciativeness, gratefulness, and thankfulness.

*Gratitude is how we thank God for getting us where we've been, where we are, and where we are going.*

He is ALWAYS listening to you, even when you're not actively praying. There are no coincidences in life—God has carefully orchestrated every step that has placed you where you are today. He wants to provide for you, and He wants to know that you recognize His guidance in your life.

Practicing gratitude does not need to take a long time. Most days, I only spend about three to five minutes showing gratitude to God. By taking just a few moments to say thank you for all that I have, I'm showing God that I see what He's doing in my life and that I'm excited and grateful for where He's taking me next.

Here are three simple ways to start incorporating gratitude into your life:

**Grab a gratitude journal** - This was the first step that I took to incorporate more gratitude into my life. There are some amazing gratitude journals out there that simply include a spot to write the date, as well as three small spaces to write three things you're grateful for that day. If you're curious which gratitude journal I use and love, head on over to teacherturnedvirtualassistant.com/resources. Each day, I challenge you to list out one thing you're thankful for from the past, present, and future.

**Make a gratitude list** - Stop what you're doing right now and go grab a pen and a sheet of paper.

Now, I want you to take five minutes and list out everything you're grateful for in your life. This list can include simple things like your pets or your house, or it can get more complex to include things like specific lessons you've learned over the years, special people in your life and why you're grateful God has placed them in your life, etc. This exercise is also a fun one to do at the end of each month to keep track of all of God's goodness throughout the year.

**Statements of gratitude** - While driving down the road, did you narrowly avoid hitting a squirrel? Take a moment to show God your gratitude. Did you have a hard conversation that you were worried wouldn't go well? Tell God thank you for giving you the words and the clarity you needed to handle the conversation well.

When it comes to gratitude, it doesn't need to take a ton of time, but it can make a huge impact. I think you'll be surprised by how far you can go just by taking the time to slow down and start incorporating gratitude into your life for 5-70 minutes a day.

## 2. START A PRAYER JOURNAL

We often come to God and ask Him for something we want, but by the time a prayer is answered, we've forgotten that we asked for it at all. When this happens, we tend to give *ourselves* the credit for achieving that goal, instead of *giving God the glory He deserves.*

Starting a prayer journal is a great way to remember your prayers. This way you can flip through your previous entries every few months and make note of which prayers God has answered. Here are a few easy ways to start using a prayer journal:

**Write freely** - You don't need to write perfectly or for long periods to get your message across. God knows exactly what you want to say, you just need to ask. Try setting a timer for 5-70 minutes and just write down whatever comes to your mind that you would like to ask Him about or that you want to process.

**Write "a year from now" letter** - This is one of my favorite exercises. Write a letter to yourself a year from now about where you want to be. Get specific. Some questions to help inspire you are:

- What is your relationship with God like?

- What does your home look or feel like?

- How are your finances? Have you paid *off* any

debt? If so, how much?

- Who are you helping/serving in your career outside of teaching?

- How is your relationship with your spouse?

- What does your motherhood look like?

- What are your kids learning?

- What are you doing to improve your health?

- What does your ideal day look like?

Once you've written your letter, refer back to it at least once a week (if not daily) to make sure you're working towards those goals!

**Make lists.** Lists are a quick way to get all your thoughts and prayers out of your head without writing in full sentences. If you're like me and don't really like the physical act of writing, this is a great option because it allows you to write out your prayers a lot faster. Some list ideas are:

- Write a list of your favorite Bible verses.

- Write out the prayers God has answered in your life.

- Write a "who I am" list.

- Write out a list of lessons you've learned.

- Write a list of questions you want to ask God.

Prayer journals can be as simple or as complicated as you want to make them. The important thing is that you use it consistently, so you can visually see how God is working in your life. I have linked the prayer journal I love in the bonus resources that I've gathered for this book, which you can access at teacherturnedvirtualassistant.com/resources.

## 3. ASK QUESTIONS

This might seem counterintuitive because God already knows what is on our hearts and minds. However, He wants us to actively seek Him out and *ask for what we want.* We need to ask Him where He wants us to go. We should question which direction He wants us to choose. We need to include Him when we're trying to make a decision.

One of my favorite ways to seek God's help is to ask Him to show me a specific sign if I'm supposed to go in one direction or another. When I started feeling the call to guide teachers out of the classroom, I asked God to show me a fox if He wanted me to pursue this nudge that I was feeling. I had never seen a fox in real life outside of a zoo, so I figured if I were to see one, I would be sure to take notice. A couple weeks later while driving home from the gym, a fox ran across the road in front of me. Thankfully I didn't hit it (I'm not sure what *that* would've meant), but I knew He was giving me the clear answer to pivot my business in that direction.

Another example is when I first felt called to write this book. I had to make a big choice about which publishing route I was going to go with. I hadn't even written the book yet, but I asked God anyway. I asked Him to show me a caterpillar if He wanted me to go one route, or a ladybug if He wanted me to go the other. I don't recall ever seeing a caterpillar or a ladybug where we live, so I thought this would be a good one to ask because it would be out of the ordinary. I also knew I had plenty of time to wait for an answer while I wrote the book.

And He answered. A few days later, I was walking into my house, and there was a big, hairy caterpillar right next to the door handle. I immediately felt chills go down my arms, and I knew which way God was calling me to go.

Here are some tips if you're asking God for a sign in your life:

- **Have patience.** You might not receive an answer right away. Sometimes God is calling us to wait patiently. That's why it's helpful to write down your questions and the signs you ask for, so you can remember them even if you have to wait awhile.

- **Watch out for the unexpected.** God might not show you the sign you asked for in the way you expect. It could show up in the changing background of your login screen on your computer. You might come across an old stuffed animal. Your child might bring home a picture they drew of that animal.

You might even see that sign in a dream.

Keep your eyes open to any possibility.

I think it's also important to remember that, sometimes, God wants us to sit in the waiting. Maybe He's preparing us to be able to handle whatever it is we're asking for. Maybe He has something even better in store. Don't get discouraged if you don't get an answer to your prayer right away. God always has three replies to our prayers:

1.  Yes

2.  Yes, but not right now

3.  I have a better plan for you.

*Prayer is the foundation.*

Whatever purpose you're trying to uncover in your life, whatever answers you're seeking, prayer is the foundation you need to build those decisions upon. We can't hope to uncover our purpose without including the One who created us—if we try, we're likely to lose our way and have to start over again.

When it comes to any big decisions in your life, we have to include God. This first P of the PURPOSE framework is one that we should come back to again and again. My hope is that you will begin implementing some (or all, if you want extra brownie points) of the prayer methods I've mentioned above and watch Him start to work in your life.

## MY PRAYER FOR YOU:

I pray that you use this time of trying to uncover your purpose to draw closer to God and seek His guidance. I pray that He shows you exactly who He has called you to become. I pray that He opens whatever doors you need to get where you're going, and that He closes any doors that might distract you. I pray that God would give you the courage to take that step of faith to follow the dreams on your heart, because He has given them to you for a reason.

## CHAPTER SUMMARY:

- You don't need to know every step of the path God is calling you toward. You just need to take that first step of faith.

- Prayer is how we draw closer to God, and it's through prayer that He can speak to us and show us exactly where He's calling us to go.

- Gratitude is how we thank God for getting us where we've been, where we are, and where we're going.

- Prayer journals are a great way to remember your prayers and keep track of which prayers God has answered.

- God wants us to actively seek Him out and ask for what we want.

- God might not answer your prayer in the way that you expect.

- Sometimes, God wants us to wait patiently for our prayers to be answered. They may not be answered right away.

- We have to actively seek God and include Him in all big decisions in our lives.

## LET ME COME ALONGSIDE YOU.

Want to dive even deeper? I've got some extra resources to share with you as you walk through this journey to uncover your purpose outside of teaching. Make sure to visit teacherturnedvirtualassistant.com/resources to access your free resources.

# CHAPTER 2:

*Uncover*

"Cast all your anxiety on him because he cares for you." 7
Peter 5:7

One of the most challenging pieces of discovering your God-given purpose outside of teaching is uncovering what giftings you already have deep down inside of you. If you've been teaching for any amount of time, I'm willing to bet you struggle with feeling like you don't have any other gifts, skills, or talents that you could turn into a career. And I'm here to tell you that's not true. If you're not sure what you would like to do outside of teaching or what you would be good at, I'm going to walk you through my four-step process, so you can start to uncover those God-given gifts inside you.

## UNCOVER STEP 1: PRAY

There's a reason prayer is the first step in the PURPOSE framework. God knows exactly who He created you to be, even if you can't see it yet yourself. Turning to Him is the quickest way to start unlocking what's been hiding inside of you. Ask God to show you what skillsets you have, and to show you how you could use those to both further His kingdom as well as to support yourself and your family.

Sometimes we sit in the "stuckness" because we're looking at ourselves through the lens of who we are now. But remember, God knows exactly who He designed you to be, and how He plans for you to get there. Rather than trying to control the situation, try turning to the God who knows and loves you so deeply that He felt compelled to create you. Ask Him for guidance in uncovering your purpose.

## UNCOVER STEP 2: ASK OTHERS

For step number two, I encourage you to select a few

special people in your life and ask them what they think your giftings are. A word of caution here—don't ask everyone you know. It's important to be discerning and only ask those who are really close to you, who know your heart inside and out, and can speak to God's giftings in your life. Some great people to ask include your parents, your closest friends, somebody who is a spiritual mentor to you, and/or someone who is where you want to be.

This doesn't have to be a super long process. There are only two key questions that I want you to ask:

1. What sets me apart from others?

2. What God-given gifts or talents do you think that I have?

The people around you see what your strengths are, even when you might not necessarily see them yourself. You might even think that everybody has the strengths that you have. *Spoiler alert: they don't.*

If you can pull these answers out of the people who've been observing you, who know you so deeply that they're going to be able to help you identify your strengths, this can be incredibly helpful in pointing you towards your purpose outside of teaching.

## UNCOVER STEP 3: PRAY (AGAIN)

Now, it's time to take what you learned in step two and confirm it with God. You don't want to just take human words at face value. You want to confirm that what they're saying is true and that it's really where God is calling you to go. Ask Him to show you your gifts. Ask Him for confirmation of what your friends, family, and mentors have told you. Ask for signs that you're on the right track. If you feel stuck with this, I encourage you to go back and read Chapter 1.

And remember, if God doesn't answer you right away, He might just be asking you to wait. Sometimes we need to be patient and know that God wants us to trust in Him. Maybe He's asking us to have patience for a reason. As you're waiting, continue to pray and take action. This isn't an excuse to sit around and do nothing while you wait for an answer from God. While you're waiting, take the action you *think* you're supposed to take, and God will eventually give you clarity.

## UNCOVER STEP 4: BELIEVE IN YOURSELF

As you read this book, I want you to know that you have the ability to pursue your dreams—*even if they seem scary.* It's so easy to get trapped in worrying about the big picture. There's a saying that goes, "How do we eat an entire elephant? One bite at a time." Sister, you do not need to try to shove the whole elephant in your mouth. Actually, that sounds kind of painful, so I'd prefer if you didn't even try. All you have to do is take small steps. You have to trust that you either already have the ability to do what you need to do, or that God is going to help you figure it out. That's what He's here for. He is here to guide us where He wants us to go. He has a plan for us. That plan was set before we were born, and all we have to do is follow in His footsteps.

## MY PRAYER FOR YOU:

I pray that God shines a light on the abilities, skills, and gifts you have that can be used to further His mission. I pray that He places people in your life that will speak love and life into you, and that will encourage you to go where He is calling you.

## CHAPTER SUMMARY:

- God knows exactly who He created you to be, even if you can't see it yet yourself. Turning to Him is the quickest way to start unlocking what's been hiding inside of you.

- Rather than trying to control the situation, try turning to the God who knows and loves you so deeply that He felt compelled to create you.

- Use discernment to figure out who you should ask about your strengths and giftings, someone who can speak to God's giftings in your life.

- Confirm what those individuals are saying is true and make sure that this is really where God is calling you to go. Ask Him for confirmation that what they've told you is true.

- You have the ability to pursue your dreams, even if they seem scary.

- Trust that either you already have the ability to do what you need to do or that God is going to help you figure it out.

## LET ME COME ALONGSIDE YOU.

Friend, I want to walk with you hand-in-hand throughout this journey of uncovering your God-given purpose outside of teaching. I've got some amazing free resources just for you. You can find them at teacherturnedvirtualassistant.com/resources.

# Teacher Turned...

# CHAPTER 3:

## *Redefine*

"The Lord himself goes before you and will be with you; he will never leave you nor forsake you. Do not be afraid; do not be discouraged."

Deuteronomy 37:8

As you work towards your goal of quitting teaching and discovering God's purpose for you outside the classroom, you might notice some thoughts like, *I'm not sure who I am outside of being a teacher* or *I've worked so many years to get to the level of success that I'm at now, am I really just going to throw it all away?*

While you're working to figure out your new God-given purpose outside of teaching, it's important to remember that God is working to transform you into the vessel capable of something even bigger. He does this by removing whatever we don't need from our lives, realigning us with His plan, and giving us everything we need to bring His mission for us to life.

During this time of transition, it's crucial that you take the time to redefine two key things about yourself: your identity and your definition of success.

## REDEFINE YOUR IDENTITY

Whether you've been a teacher for 20 years or you just started, being a teacher quickly becomes a part of your identity. Think about it—when you first meet someone, what is one of the first questions they ask you? "So, what do you do?" As soon as you answer that you're a teacher, it becomes not only how you identify yourself, but it also becomes a part of how others identify you as well.

When my students in the Teacher Turned Virtual Assistant program take the leap to quit teaching, or are considering doing so, they often struggle with what to identify themselves as, and this can really stress them out. Many of them don't want to be known as "just" a stay-at-home-mom (not that there is anything wrong with that, but this is an internal battle that many of my students and myself have faced). They still want the piece of their identity that helps others outside the home in some capacity. They want the piece of their identity that was impacting the world positively and making a difference.

If you're anything like my TTVA students (which if you're reading this book, I know you are), you have to alter your thinking of who you are, both in God's eyes and your own. For me personally, I had to understand that I wasn't meant to teach forever, and that God had me go through that experience for a reason and a season. It took me awhile to realize that I could keep my identity as a teacher, but it could be changed to mean something different than teaching children in a classroom. Let me break down both of these ideas for you.

**Clarify who you are in God's eyes** - It's easy to get stuck in your head worrying about who you are and who you're meant to become, but let's not forget to seek those answers from the One who created us. God created you on purpose, with a purpose, and for a purpose. The first thing you need to do is identify yourself in the way that He sees you.

My favorite way to do this is with God-centered "I am" statements. These are short sentences that break down exactly who you are in God's eyes. These "I am" statements allow you to be who you desire to become because of God's power that is being spoken into you. Some examples of "I am" statements include:

- I am chosen. (John 75:76 and Deuteronomy 74:2)

- I am a child of God. (Romans 8:77 and Galatians 3:26)

- I am a new creation. (2 Corinthians 5:77)

- I am loved. (Jeremiah 37:3)

- I am redeemed. (Galatians 3:73 and Romans 3:24)

- I am accepted. (Romans 75:7)

- I am unique. (Psalm 739:73)

- I am created for a purpose. (Jeremiah 29:77)

- I am special. (Ephesians 2:70)

- I am important. (7 Peter 2:9)

- I am empowered. (Philippians 4:73)

- I am protected. (Psalm 727:3)

I challenge you to choose 70 of the "I am" statements above, or search the Bible for any statements that speak to you. Write them down, and put them somewhere where you can read them each and every day. I love reading mine as part of my morning routine because it starts my day off on such a beautiful note.

**Change what being a teacher means to you** - Quitting teaching doesn't mean that you'll no longer be a teacher. You can definitely still teach, impact, and change the lives of others—just in a different capacity. Maybe God's calling you to teach others how to live a healthier life, to get more organized, or to connect with others on a deeper level. Maybe He wants you to help others learn how to manage their bookkeeping, launch their course, or design a website that speaks to their dream customers. What if He wants you to impact more people through serving a business that has a God-centered mission?

All these things use key components of teaching, just in a different way. Teachers have amazing skills that can be adapted for almost any type of job, including:

1. **Customer service skills -** As teachers, we juggle conversations with parents, admin, staff, and even our students. We settle disputes, compromise, and referee arguments. These are all great skills that can be used in other job environments.

2. **The willingness to learn new things -** When we're teaching and we get thrown a new technique that is said to help our students, we're going to learn everything we can about it and implement it, so we can improve our students' learning, their lives, and ours. This willingness to learn is an incredibly beneficial skill in any career.

3. **The ability to adapt -** Teachers know: no two students are the same, and a majority of the time our lesson plans go out the window when it's

actually time to teach. As a teacher, your ability to adapt and change your plans is what sets you apart from people in other industries.

I truly believe that teachers are amazing at anything they choose to do because of the skills I mentioned above. I've seen these skills in my students that are in the Teacher Turned Freelancer Academy, and I've seen them in other teachers I know that have quit teaching. We all have these skills inherent in us, and there are so many jobs and businesses out there that could use our skills and abilities to improve the lives of many others.

It's also important to make sure that any career path you're pursuing actually aligns with your values and the type of life you want to live. Try making a list of ideal career characteristics to help you stay on track with where you want to end up. Some examples might include the level of schedule flexibility, opportunities for growth, and even the amount of flexibility for how you get the job done. Admittedly, I'm bias towards entrepreneurship options like becoming a Virtual Assistant because it gives you the freedom to build your business as a side hustle while you're still teaching, and there's also no cap on income. If you'd like to learn more about becoming a Virtual Assistant to see if this might be a good fit for you, I invite you to check out my free workshop at ariannavernier.com/free-workshop.

## REDEFINE YOUR DEFINITION OF SUCCESS

A lot of people think that success means they've accomplished something amazing, but I don't believe that to be the case. I don't think anyone wakes up one day and says, "I did it! I'm officially successful!" Success isn't a destination that we're going to arrive at in 75 or 20 years. It's this thinking that leaves people constantly striving for more, stressing that they're not enough, and feeling burnt out.

Success is about enjoying the journey. It's about being fully present wherever you are, and giving 700% to whatever God has called you to be in that moment. It's about aligning all areas of your life with exactly who He designed you to become.

Sister, I want you to know this-God doesn't want you

running the hamster wheel we like to call life. He wants you to slow down and be purposeful and intentional in every area of your life. He wants you to be a patient and present mother, a loving spouse, a dedicated daughter, a devoted Christian. He doesn't care what milestones you've hit. He cares that you are who He's created you to be.

Take a moment to write down what you feel equals true success. Try to be as specific as possible. This may take some time, but that's okay. It's important that you build a life that reflects success as it looks in your eyes, not the world's version.

## MY PRAYER FOR YOU:

I pray that this chapter gives you the permission you've been seeking to let go of old identities and transform into the woman God has called you to become. I pray that it helps you understand that these earthly titles are not your identity, but your identity is found in who He says you are.

## CHAPTER SUMMARY:

- God created you on purpose, with a purpose, and for a purpose.

- You need to identify yourself in the way that God sees you.

- Using God-centered "I am" statements will allow you to become who you desire because of His power that is being spoken into you.

- You can still teach, impact, and change the lives of others-just in a different capacity.

- Teachers have amazing skills that can be adapted for almost any type of job or business.

- Success isn't a destination that we're going to arrive at in 75 or 20 years.

- Success is about aligning all areas of your life with exactly who God has designed you to be.

**LET ME COME ALONGSIDE YOU.**

I'd love to keep the purpose party going and connect with you even further. I've got some extra resources to share with you as you walk through this journey to uncover your purpose outside of teaching. Make sure to visit teacherturnedvirtualassistant.com/resources to access your free resources.

Teacher Turned...

# CHAPTER 4:

## Prioritize

"In their hearts humans plan their course, but the Lord establishes their steps."

Proverbs 76:9

"I want to do ____, but I just don't have the time."

It's an excuse I hear over and over again. The same excuse that leaves people stuck where they are, wishing they could follow the dreams that God has placed on their hearts but wondering how they're ever going to be able to do them with everything else on their plate.

Friend, you've hung out with me for four chapters

now, and I think it's about time for a bit of a tough-love moment. I want you to remember that *if something truly matters, you'll make time for it.*

Look, I get that being a teacher, a mom, and a woman in general means that your plate is overflowing with never-ending to-do lists, and by the time your head hits the pillow each night, you're exhausted and stressed over having to do it all again the next day.

But what if God is challenging you to lay down some of those to-dos and instead pursue the dream that He has blessed you with? What if He's asking you to take a step of faith, set aside what doesn't really matter, and pursue what does?

If you want to get to the land that God has waiting for you, you can't stay stuck in the wilderness of where you are now. I don't know about you, but I really don't want to be wandering around trying to figure out my purpose for 40 years like the people of Israel did (See Numbers 14:34).

Let's face it, you're not going to find another second in your day if you keep going the way that you are. We need to prioritize our time and give it to what really matters-our faith, our families, and the calling that God has given us. There are two key ways that we can learn how to delegate time each day to the things in our lives that count, and I want to share those with you.

## AUDIT YOUR TIME

The first step toward finding more time in your day in order to pursue your God-given purpose is by doing a time audit. I'm going to challenge you to take a good, hard look at where you are spending (or wasting) your time, and where you could adjust things in your life in order to find pockets of time to start your journey out of teaching.

If you really tried, could you find the time? I want you to take a moment to sit down and analyze your life, and ask yourself, "Where am I hemorrhaging time? Where am I wasting it? What could I do better with my time?" Could you then find the time you need to pursue your goals?

*There are two kinds of people in this world: those with reasons and those with results.*
*- Alan Kohen*

If you're determined to hold on to the life that you already have, being stuck in the classroom but not being fulfilled in it, then you can absolutely keep all your reasons or excuses of why you can't find the time to pursue God's purpose for you. However, if you're ready to start making changes today that will lead you towards creating your dream life outside of teaching, then your next step is to take a serious look at how you can use your time more effectively.

For the next seven days, I'm going to challenge you to do a time audit. I want you to write down every single thing you do from the moment you get up until the time you go to bed. I recommend keeping track in a document on your phone, since you're likely to always have that with you. I want you to be as specific as possible. For example, I might write down that from 7:78 AM to 7:48 AM, I was scrolling Instagram. Then I would continue to do that for everything I did throughout the day and repeat that for seven days.

The biggest challenge with this task is not altering your usual activities and being honest with yourself. If you usually scroll on your phone for two hours a day, don't cut that out during this exercise. You want an honest look at how you're actually using your time, so just do what you usually do

48

and then write it down in your time audit document.

At the end of those seven days, I want you to sit down and total up how much time you spent each day in the different categories of your life—whether that's for your marriage, your kids, your job, mindless scrolling, errands, etc.

Now, I want you to analyze which areas of your life you're spending time in *unintentionally*. Notice I didn't say "where you're spending the most time." If you're spending the most time *intentionally* pouring into your kids, I believe that's time well spent. But if you're consistently looking up from your phone wondering where the last 45 minutes went, that's unintentional time wasted.

Keep an eye out for these five popular time-sucks:

1. **Social media -** If you are spending 30 minutes a day scrolling through social media, that's 782 hours a year. Do you see where that time could be used more effectively? If you notice that you're spending a lot of time mindlessly scrolling on social media, I want you to ask yourself what it would look like if, instead of browsing through Instagram as soon as you wake up, you hopped on your laptop and spent

half an hour looking for new positions outside of teaching that align with you. Or, maybe you're trying to build your true passion as a side-hustle while you're still teaching. What if, instead of scrolling, you spent those 30 minutes working on an income-generating task that will take you one step closer to quitting teaching?

2. **Checking your email -** I also like to call this "putting out fires." Maybe you constantly find yourself checking your email 20 times a day, worrying about a student's parents emailing you, or looking out for an email from admin. What if you set one specific time to check your email each day? You could dedicate 20 minutes at lunchtime or right before you leave the classroom at the end of the day to just knock it all out, instead of eating up your mental energy as well as your time.

3. **Watching TV -** I'm not saying you need to give up all your relaxation time of watching your favorite shows. I am saying you should plan intentional time to watch one or two shows instead of binging a whole series as a way to avoid anything else.

4. **Errands -** Do you find yourself running 70 million errands throughout the week? How could you condense them down? Could you order some stuff online so that you don't have to spend time at the store? Could you give yourself one 2-hour block each week to knock out all your errands?

5. **Meal planning/prepping -** How much time are you spending figuring out what to eat each week? Could you spend one day making a bunch of meals, that way you don't have to spend that time every other day making a new meal or heating it up? If you've already got the meal made, your family members can heat it up for themselves. Or could you delegate meal planning to a family member two to three nights a week?

Now listen, sister, I'm not saying you have to cut all these things out of your day. You definitely deserve some time to relax and unwind. But when you take a hard look at where you're hemorrhaging your time, I'm fairly certain that you'll find chunks of wasted time that you could reduce down or remove altogether and dedicate to your journey out of the classroom.

I'd also like to note that if you complete this time audit and tell me, "Arianna, I really don't have the time. I'm going all day long." Then I have one thing to tell you—you're doing too much.

*When you say 'yes' to something, you're saying 'no' to something else.*
*—Robin Sharma*

If you're saying "yes" to too many different things, but not the things that are the most important to you—like spending time with your kids or pursuing your God-given purpose—*then you're saying "no" to the most important things.*

If you really can't find time anywhere in your day to build your dream life, maybe it's time to start saying "no" to some things that are less important. Instead of saying, "I wish I had the time to do ____," I want you to flip the script and say, "Where could I make the time to do this? Because this is so important to me."

It would be easy to simply read this section of the book and continue on, but I want to hold you accountable to actually complete this audit of your time. I challenge you to take a screenshot of your time audit and post it in Ditch the Classroom community (facebook.com/groups/ditchtheclassroom), so I can celebrate with you as you complete this challenge.

## CREATE A PLAN

I want to remind you that you don't need to eat the whole elephant at once. Many times, we think we don't have the time to hit a big goal, so we don't even try. What if instead, we broke our goal down into bite-size chunks and planned out time each week to accomplish those smaller tasks?

I want you to take a moment, grab a piece of paper, and write this down: *if it's important enough, I'll make the time. If not, I'll make an excuse.* Post this paper somewhere where you can see it multiple times a day.

You have to prioritize what is important to you and spend your time intentionally on those things. You need to have a plan for how to spend your time each day.

The best way to do this is by using a planner and planning out your week. I recommend using a paper planner, and you can find my favorite planner over at teacherturnedvirtualassistant.com/resources. Studies have shown that when you write something down, you're much more likely to remember it and accomplish it. The biggest argument I hear from the women I serve is that they don't like using a planner because it makes them feel stuck and like they have no flexibility. I think the opposite is true. When you use a planner, you're getting everything out of your brain so that you have more freedom and space in your brain. A planner is not meant to be a dictator. It's meant to be a guide that supports you in accomplishing the things that are most important to you.

Now, looking at a blank planner each week can be somewhat overwhelming, so let me guide you through seven steps for filling out your planner.

**Step I: Make time for your faith** - Time with God is the number one priority. We can't expect to get clear on our purpose if we're not spending time growing closer to the One who gave us that purpose. Write down the time each day that you're going to spend praying, reading your Bible, or just sitting in His presence. This doesn't have to take a ton of time—even 15 minutes would be amazing! I love spending my time with God in the mornings, but you could also do it in the evening after the kids go to bed or in the middle of the day as a bit of a "breath of fresh air" in your hectic schedule.

**Step 2: Prioritize your family** - Of course, family comes next. Plan in that intentional date night with your spouse, time focused on each of your kids, or any family activities that are on the calendar. Make sure your family is prioritized in your schedule by plugging those events into your planner.

**Step 3: Focus on your health** - You can't expect to have any energy for the things in your life that truly matter if you're not prioritizing your health. Exercise and meal planning/prepping should be the next items added into your planner.

**Step 4: Pursue your purpose** - I know what you're thinking: *An entire book about purpose, yet it's the fourth in the list for planning my week?!*This book is not only about discovering your purpose outside of teaching, but it's also about *living your life more intentionally and doing the things that really matter to* *you.* So, after you've fit in your time with God, your family, and your health, then you're going to plan in time to pursue God's purpose for you. Do you have a one-hour block three days a week that you could dedicate to this? *Great!* Do you have one night a week that your spouse can be in charge of dinner and bedtime, so you can spend four solid hours focusing on tasks that will draw you closer to your goal of quitting teaching? *That's awesome.* Block that into your planner.

**Step 5: Plan in the "extras"** -_Extra things in your to-do list that don't fit into one of the four categories above are just that—extra tasks that don't really make a big impact on your overall life. Those should go into your planner last, and only if there's room. One way to prioritize the order of tackling such tasks would be to write them all in a list. Write a "1" next to the ones that are most pertinent—maybe they have a due date they need to be done by or are just driving you crazy. Write a "2" next to the extra tasks that are somewhat important but that don't have a specific deadline. Write a "3" next to the tasks that aren't really that important. I recommend giving yourself a two-hour time block each week to dedicate to these tasks. During that time, focus on accomplishing as much as you can, starting with the 1s on the list and working through to the 2s and 3s as you have time. If not, those can wait until next week.

**Step 6: Make time for white space** - One of the biggest excuses I hear about why women don't want to use a planner is because they spend all this time planning out their week, then something happens, and it all goes down the drain. I want you to remember—the pieces of your day don't have to stay in their exact time frames. It's okay if things end up getting shuffled around a bit. This is a reason that I recommend keeping some white space in your day, that way you can adjust your schedule if needed. And if you don't need to adjust, then you have earned yourself some time to sit on your butt and chill.

**Step 7: Check for alignment** - You need to check and make sure that the tasks you have planned in your week are ultimately getting you to where you want to be, or better yet, where God is calling you to go. Look at every task that you wrote in your planner and ask yourself, "Are these tasks helping me prioritize my faith, family, or my health? Are these tasks allowing me to live my life intentionally? Are they helping me pursue my God-given purpose? Is my schedule allowing me to dedicate the time I'm going to need to be able to do that?" If the answer to any of those questions is no, then it's time to delete that task or delegate it to someone else. You have to make sure that you're creating a life that you love every day—one that is in alignment with where God wants you to be.

## MY PRAYER FOR YOU:

I pray that God would show you where you're using your time unintentionally. I pray that He opens your eyes and helps you dedicate your time to those things in your life that are precious to you, like your family, your faith, and your God-given purpose. I ask that He remove anything from your life that isn't needed, so you can go where He is calling you to go.

## CHAPTER SUMMARY:

- If something truly matters, you'll make time for it.

- What if God is challenging you to lay down some of your to-dos and instead pursue the dream that He has blessed you with?

- Take a good look at where you are spending (or wasting) your time, and where you could adjust things in your life in order to find pockets of time to start your journey out of teaching.

- Planning out your week allows you to intentionally use your time to pour into the things that matter most.

## LET ME COME ALONGSIDE YOU.

I'd love to help you make time to pursue your purpose outside of teaching. I've got some amazing free resources just for you, which you can find over at teacherturnedvirtualassistant.com/resources.

# Teacher Turned...

# CHAPTER 5:

## Overcome

" Cast all your anxiety on Him because He cares for you."

1 Peter 5:7

As you're working toward leaving teaching and pursuing God's calling on your life, you're going to face some roadblocks. Some of these will be external, coming from those around you. Some will be internal, coming from the place inside of you that wants things to stay the way that they are, to stay safe in the security of what you know.

Before we dive into the four main challenges you may face, I want you to take a moment to shift your mindset about them. Instead of seeing any of these obstacles as hindering your journey, I want you to see them for what they are—challenges that can be overcome when God is by your side. Maybe He's put this road block in front of you as a test of your faith. Maybe He wants to see if you trust Him enough to turn to Him when you're struggling. Whatever the case, if we can reframe our mindset around these inevitable hiccups, we stand a much better chance of overcoming them.

## ROADBLOCK #1: GUILT

So many of the teachers I talk to who want to quit teaching battle major guilt about letting their families down or "wasting" their teaching degrees. I totally understand, because I felt the same way. Let's break both of these down:

**<u>Guilt about letting your family down</u>** – Listen friend, I get it. You don't want to "let others down," especially those who may have helped you get your teaching degree in the first place. But I want you to understand one key thing: other people's expectations are not your responsibility. We can't live our lives constantly trying to seek the validation and approval of others. It will never happen, and it's too exhausting to even try.

If someone close to you is expressing concern about your choice to pursue a new purpose outside of the classroom, they're most likely only saying these things to you for one of 3 reasons:

1. **Their own fears -** People often push their fears onto others. They're probably not even aware that they're doing it. Remember that this is a battle that they're facing internally, and you don't need to take it on as well.

2. **Their own unhappiness -** Do you remember the age-old saying: "A person who is drowning will try to take someone down with them"? People want to feel like they have others with them in the struggle. They don't want to feel like they're being left behind to deal with their unhappiness themselves. Again, they might not realize that they're doing it, but those that you love might be expressing concerns about you quitting teaching simply because they're also unhappy with where they're at but are too afraid to do anything about it.

3. **Fear for your safety-** Let's face it, the people in our

lives who matter the most to us want to know that we're safe and cared for. When we step into new territory and out of the identity in which others have known us, that can trigger the need for people to feel like they have to protect us.

So, what can you say to those that you love if they cause you to feel guilty about your choice to leave teaching? My favorite response is, "Thank you for your concern, but this is my life, and this dream has been given to me for a reason. I don't want to regret not following it." You've shown them that you see where they're coming from, but you've firmly stated that this is your journey, not theirs. I also want you to remember that *YOU DON'T NEED ANYONE'S PERMISSION* to pursue your God-given purpose outside of teaching.

*If God has told you to go. Then don't let others' fear hold you back.*

**<u>Guilt around not using your teaching degree anymore</u> -**
So many of the teachers I talk to feel guilty about
leaving the students behind, and this is another form of
guilt that I completely understand. Again, we need to
reframe our mind about it. What if you're still able to
change the lives of kids, but just in a different capacity?
What if instead of only impacting the lives of 30
students a year, you were able to reach hundreds
through whatever calling God has placed on your
heart? What if you're meant to use that teaching
degree to help others learn a crucial skill that would
allow them to go out and impact hundreds more? We
don't have to stick ourselves in a box called "the
classroom." We can use our teaching degrees in many
different ways, and still make the world a better place
while doing so.

## ROADBLOCK #2: IMPOSTER SYNDROME

Everyone deals with imposter syndrome, but not
many people know that it actually has a name. Many people
don't even recognize that the fears they're struggling with are

just imposter syndrome rearing its ugly head. Before we jump into three ways to overcome imposter syndrome, let's define it.

According to Google, imposter syndrome is a psychological pattern in which an individual doubts their skills, talents, or accomplishments, and has a persistent, internalized fear of being exposed as a fraud. So essentially, imposter syndrome makes you feel like you're a fake. It might make you wonder, *Who am I to do this?* or *Why is someone paying ME for this when that person over there has so much more experience?*

Seventy-five percent of people are said to experience imposter syndrome—even executives, CEOs, and celebrities experience these feelings. I'm also willing to bet that the 25% who say they don't experience imposter syndrome just simply don't know how to identify their feelings. It's a constant battle for so many, but it's another that can be overcome if you have the right tools in your pocket.

**Combat strategy I: Positive affirmations** - Positive affirmations are simple statements that can help you reframe your beliefs about what you can do. These affirmations should be statements that you believe about yourself already or that you believe *could* happen. Some examples are:

- I'm caring towards others.

- I have a great attention to detail.

- People's lives are changed when they work with me.

I recommend writing your affirmations on a piece of paper that you can reference whenever you're doubting yourself. This will help you flip the switch from "I have no idea what I'm doing. Why did I quit teaching to do this?" to "Okay, I'm struggling with feeling like a fraud, but even though I may not know how to do this thing, I know that I'm really good at these other things, and I know that with time I can practice and figure out this thing I'm not yet feeling confident in."

**Combat strategy 2: Create a "feel good" folder -**

A "feel good" folder is a great way to battle thoughts of doubt and fear. I recommend creating a folder in your phone with screenshots of positive emails, texts, comments, and even projects that you feel like you did a good job on. You probably have your phone on you most of the time, so this is a quick way to be able to go read through things that make you feel more confident. Like positive affirmations, you're just reminding yourself, "I have the ability to figure things out. Maybe I didn't know how to do this before, but now this person is telling me they love what I did for them, and I was able to figure it out."

**Combat strategy 3: Practice. practice. practice –**

It's cliche to say, but practice makes perfect. If someone wants to pay you to do something for them, try doing it for yourself first. YouTube and Google are your best friends. Nobody has to know that a project you created was for a fictitious client or job. They just want to know that you can do it, period. Start practicing before anyone even hires you, and you'll build that confidence to go for it when they do.

Sister, you have the ability to figure things out. You don't have to sit in fear of the unknown, and you don't have to struggle with feeling like a fraud. When you face these thoughts (and you will), I want you to say this to yourself: "The fears in my head are not true—they're just a prison that I've placed myself in. I can choose to believe something different each day."

## ROADBLOCK #3: PERFECTIONISM

One of the biggest struggles I see so many teachers face is that they feel like they need to do things perfectly. Friend, let me say this up front—done is better than perfect. You can always improve anything you're working on, so if you're not taking action because you think whatever you're doing has to be perfect, it's never going to happen.

*"Farmers who wait for perfect weather never plant. If they watch every cloud, they never harvest."*
*- Ecclesiastes 11:4*

When I'm battling perfection, I like to ask myself, "What would happen if I didn't put this out into the world? What if God meant for this to change someone's life, but I sat on it instead?" You won't always know that whatever you're putting out into the world is what the world actually wants. But remember—you can always tweak things as you go. Choose to take that step of faith and do whatever it is that

God is calling you to do, even if it's not 100% perfect.

## ROADBLOCK #4: DISTRACTIONS

Sometimes we know God is calling us, yet we're afraid to answer. We wonder if we're hearing God right, whether He is really choosing us. We wonder if now is the right time or if we should wait just a little longer. So, instead, we distract ourselves with things that we think are important or give excuses about why we can't answer God's call right away.

*Delayed disobedience is*
*Still disobedience.*

When we don't take immediate action on God's calling, we're missing out on His blessings and protections. Sometimes our call from God feels uncomfortable, the timing feels off, or it feels inconvenient. This is how obedience is tested. As chosen daughters of the King, we need to make sure our priorities are in check and that we have a willing spirit.

Instead of waiting on the right time or continuing to delay answering God's call, we are directed in scripture to take immediate action. When Jesus asked Simon Peter to join him, Simon Peter immediately got out of his fishing boat and began to follow Christ (See Matthew 4:18). He didn't know the outcome. He didn't know "how." He only knew that God told him to come. We have to put aside our fears, worries, and excuses. Instead, we need to follow God's lead, so we can bring glory to Him.

When you take immediate action on God's calling, it will bring you favor, blessing, and—most importantly—closeness to God. God promises that His children will be blessed, as well as their children, and their children's children. When you walk in obedience and answer God's calling, you will reap heavenly rewards and change the path of your life.

As we close out this chapter, I want you to remember that God gave you the dream that has been placed on your heart for a reason. You can either let Him tap you with a feather and obey immediately, or He can hit you over the head with a large book because you're not listening. Which one would you prefer?

## MY PRAYER FOR YOU:

I pray you open your heart to answer God's call and know that He is with you, encouraging you, blessing you, and protecting you on your journey. I know that walking out God's plans for you will be the greatest honor of your life. I pray that God helps you overcome any obstacles that are placed in your path, so you can go where He is calling you.

## CHAPTER SUMMARY:

- As you pursue God's calling on your life, you're going to face internal and external road blocks.

- All challenges can be overcome when God is by your side.

- If someone close to you is expressing concern about your choice to pursue a new purpose outside of the classroom, they're most likely doing so because of their own fears, unhappiness, or concern for your safety.

- When God tells you to go, don't let the fears of others hold you back.

- We can use our teaching degree to impact the world in so many ways.

- Imposter syndrome makes you feel like you're a fraud, but it can be overcome by implementing a few simple strategies.

- Done is better than perfect.

- Delayed obedience is still disobedience.

- When you take immediate action on God's calling, it will bring you favor, blessing, and closeness to God.

## LET ME COME ALONGSIDE YOU.

Want to dive even deeper? I've got some extra resources to share with you as you walk through this journey to uncover your purpose outside of teaching. Make sure to visit teacherturnedvirtualassistant.com/resources to access your free resources.

# CHAPTER 6:

## Set Goals

"The Lord makes firm the steps of the one who delights in Him; though he may stumble, he will not fall, for the Lord upholds him with His hand."

Psalm 37:23-24

Once you get the "Go!" from God, it's time to take action. Even if you're not 700% positive on the direction He's asking you to go, God loves to see you stepping out in faith and will give you more clarity as you move forward.

However, it is important to remember the difference between taking bold steps of faith versus just trying to do what we think we need to do. If we want God to have control of the steering wheel of our lives, we can't be trying to yank that steering wheel over to the passenger side every chance we get. Remember to walk with God and turn to Him in prayer as you're setting your goals.

The best way to start working towards bringing God's purpose for you to life is by setting goals and taking small steps to work toward achieving those goals every day. There are two processes we need to figure out what our goals actually are and to break down how to actually make them happen.

## BACKWARD DESIGN

In teaching, we have to figure out what skills our students need to master and then work backwards to figure out how we're going to help them get from where they are to where they need to be. This is called "backward design." The same can be done with identifying our goals. We can start with where we want to be and then identify what we need to do to get there. Let's walk through the three steps for how to backward design your goals.

## Step #1: Determine what your income goal is -

The first thing you need to do in setting goals is figure out exactly what income goal you need to achieve. You want to make this goal attainable—I don't recommend making your first income goal: "Hit $100k." If you set it too far out, it's going to take you a lot longer to reach that goal, and there are more chances that you could give up because you might not feel like it's *actually* possible.

A great starting goal is to replace your teaching income. This way you don't have to worry about providing for your family once you quit teaching and can fully focus on doing what God has called you to do. Once you have this number, write it down on a piece of paper.

## Step #2: Set your monthly goal –

Now you need to take your income goal and divide that number by 12 in order to get your monthly goal. For example, if your income goal is $60k, your monthly goal would be $5k. You will know exactly what you need to earn each month in order to hit your larger annual income goal.

### Step #3: Identify what you need to do to hit that monthly goal -

Now you need to figure out the number of clients you would need or how many products you would need to sell in order to hit that monthly income goal. Write that number down on the same piece of paper. This will vary depending on what you're charging for whatever service or product you've created, so this is also something you would need to identify.

For example, if your income goal is $5,000 and you charge $500 for a specific service that you offer, you would need 70 clients to hit that income goal. If you charge $7000, you would only need 5 clients to achieve that goal.

*Bonus tip:* If you're charging too low, and you would need 75 clients a month to hit that monthly goal, then you need to raise your prices!

## 90-DAY GOAL SETTING

My friends and family often wonder how I'm able to get so much done in my life and business while wrangling two children under three. It's no secret—I set attainable 90-day goals and map out the exact steps I need to do to get there.

Once you've identified your big 90-day goal, write it down at the top of a piece of paper. Underneath your goal, I want you to list out everything you would need to do in order to accomplish that goal, no matter how big or small it is. It might take you a couple days to come up with the full list, which is totally fine. The point is to brain dump everything you would need to do, in whatever order it comes out of your head. You should try to be as specific as possible so that you can remember what you meant when you refer back to this list.

For example, when I sat down to write this book, I knew that my big goal was to complete it in 3 months. With 9 chapters total, I knew that I wanted to write one chapter a week. But I couldn't just jump in with no plan, so I also added to my list, "Create book outline." I also wanted you to have resources to help guide you along this journey, so I added a task for that to my list as well.

Once you've got your list, I want you to make a table with 3 columns on your sheet of paper. Label the columns "Month 1", "Month 2", and "Month 3". It should look something like this:

| Month 1 | Month 2 | Month 3 |
| --- | --- | --- |
| | | |

Now you're going to take your list from before and organize the items into the order that they need to be completed. I recommend starting with the tasks that need to be completed first and placing them into the "Month 1" column. Next, move to any tasks that would need to be completed last, and add them to the "Month 3" column. Then, you can take a look at what tasks are left and place them in whichever column makes the most sense.

Once you've got your tasks organized, you've officially got a game plan for exactly what steps you need to take to achieve that goal and in what order you need to do them. You can also take this exercise a step further and break each month down into weekly goals and even daily goals. This is a process that I have each of my students in the Teacher Turned Virtual Assistant program work through, and those women who take the time to sit down and follow this process are typically the ones that have been the most successful in their journey out of teaching.

Don't forget to communicate your goals with others in your life. Communication is the key to everything, and it's how you'll be able to feel supported by the people you love. Make sure you tell your husband, your kids, your family, and your friends what your goals are. Tell them how they can support you in achieving those goals. Does your husband need to be in charge of cooking dinner for the next few weeks so you can dedicate that time to your goals? Do you need your mom to come over and watch your kids a few hours a week so you can accomplish the tasks you've written down? Communicate those needs!

*A year from now, you will wish you had started today.*
*-Karen Lamb*

As we wrap up this chapter, it's important to remember that action builds momentum. When we look at our big goals as a whole, it's really easy to get overwhelmed. But again, we're not trying to eat that entire elephant at once. We need to break it down into bite-size steps that are easy to implement and then take action each day to accomplish what we set out to do.

## MY PRAYER FOR YOU:

I pray that God would give you direction in figuring out what your goals should be and what steps that you need to take to get there. I pray that He would guide you where He wants you to go, that He sees your steps of faith, and rewards you abundantly for them.

## CHAPTER SUMMARY:

- In order to start working towards God's purpose in your life, you need to take small steps to work toward achieving those goals every day.

- It's important to backward design your goals, so you

have a clear picture of where you want to be and can then identify what you need to do to get there.

- The key to achieving your goals is breaking them down into bite-size steps that are easy to implement.

## LET ME COME ALONGSIDE YOU.

Sister, I know God has a purpose for you and I want to walk with you hand-in-hand to figure out what that is. I've got some amazing free resources just for you. You can find them at teacherturnedvirtualassistant.com/resources.

# CHAPTER 7:

## *Evaluate*

"For I know the plans I have for you," declares the Lord. "Plans to prosper you and not to harm you. Plans to give you hope & a future."

Jeremiah 29:11

Sister, we've walked through a lot together throughout the course of this book. But none of it matters if you don't take the time to assess and evaluate each step to make sure you're in alignment with where you want to go, or more importantly, *where God is calling you to go.*

One of my biggest fears about quitting teaching was that I would look up in the future and not like where I was any better than that classroom. That fear came to life just six months into my journey out of teaching.

When God first showed me that I was supposed to become a Virtual Assistant, I immediately jumped in and plowed forward. I worked with anyone who would hire me, offering services I didn't necessarily enjoy, for a lot less than I should have charged, all while trying to juggle a newborn and the struggles of becoming a new mom. I thought that if I just did a little more, worked a little harder, lived on a little less sleep, that I would reach my goals faster.

A few months into my journey, God gave me the wake-up call I needed. I had a few clients that were not a good fit and found myself with a client who expected me to work on Christmas day—something I didn't even have to do when I was teaching! I looked at what I had built the last few months, and I cried out to God that this was not what I had in mind.

Do you notice what was missing in those first few months of my journey? Looking back, I can see it so clearly. Once I got the "Go!" from God, I took the reins and ran. I didn't turn to Him to help me figure out who I was meant to serve.

I didn't put Him first or even my family first, thinking I had to hustle to get where I wanted to go.

After that Christmas day, I took a long, hard look at where I had veered off path. I released control of my business to God, let go of those clients who weren't in line with where He wanted me to be, and partnered with Him to figure out what He actually wanted me to do. Within a few months, I found myself working a lot less, working with businesses whose missions I so fully believed in, spending more time with my sweet new baby girl, and started mentoring moms and teachers who were facing the same struggles I had faced.

Oftentimes, we ask God to get us where He wants us to go, but we have our hands so firmly grasped on the steering wheel that we're tugging against Him. In those instances, God will usually let us take the reins back, so we can learn the valuable lesson that His plans are greater than ours.

Since that moment, I've consistently taken time to stop and assess where I am and where God wants me to go, making sure the two align with each other. Sometimes, if you don't take a moment to make sure you're on the path you intended, you might look up and realize you're on a different route altogether.

The best way to assess whether you're working towards God's purpose for you is to walk back through each of the steps I've taken you through in this book. Below, I've compiled a checklist that will help you check for alignment, and if you ever find yourself veering away from it, you'll know what you need to do to find that path again.

But, before we do that, sweet friend, I want to remind you of the most important thing to remember when pursuing your purpose—*God has your back.*

This doesn't mean that everything is going to be peaches and roses throughout your whole journey. Sometimes God puts us through certain situations to test our faith in Him. It does mean that, even though we may face struggles, we can remain confident in the knowledge that God has gone before us and is paving our path. So, before you utilize the checklist below, I want you to always remember to turn to God's help first.

*He's got you.*

## ALIGNMENT CHECKLIST:

- [ ] Am I consistently turning to God in prayer along this journey?

- [ ] Does He intentionally have me in a waiting season so that I can grow my faith in Him?

- [ ] Have I shown Him gratitude for the things He has already given me?

- [ ] Am I keeping a prayer journal so that I can keep track of God's answered prayers in my life?

- [ ] Do I consistently ask for God's guidance and direction when I'm faced with a decision?

- [ ] Have I taken the time to ask those I trust what my strengths are because I might not directly see them?

- [ ] Do I believe that God is guiding me and will equip me along the way, even if I don't know all of the answers up front?

- ☐ Am I still holding on to things that used to be a part of my identity but that no longer represent who I am?

- ☐ Have I taken the time to identify who I am in Christ?

- ☐ Am I focusing too much on the world's version of success?

- ☐ Am I utilizing my time effectively?

- ☐ Do I have a plan to help me keep in alignment?

- ☐ Am I letting guilt from others hold me back?

- ☐ Am I utilizing the techniques I've learned in this book to overcome any feelings of imposter syndrome?

- ☐ Is perfectionism hindering my forward momentum?

- ☐ What distractions are derailing me?

- ☐ Have I identified my goals?

- ☐ Do I have a game plan full of bite-sized tasks that will help me achieve those goals?

If you find that you're hung up at any point in this checklist, then it's time to go back to that section of the book and dive deeper into uncovering the roadblock. This book is not meant for you to read once and then leave it on your shelf collecting dust. It's meant to be a living, breathing tool for you to use consistently in your journey to figuring out God's purpose for you. Use it this way and watch the magic unfold.

## MY PRAYER FOR YOU:

I pray that God would make your path clear, and that, even though you may face speedbumps along the way, He will be there to guide you. God knows that you are capable of amazing things, and I pray that He will steer you back toward your true purpose if you ever start to veer off-course.

## CHAPTER SUMMARY:

- You need to consistently check to make sure you're in alignment with where God is calling you to go.

- If you find yourself off track, use the alignment checklist to help you get back on the right path.

**LET ME COME ALONGSIDE YOU.**

Want to dive even deeper? I've got some extra resources to share with you as you walk through this journey to uncover your purpose outside of teaching. Make sure to visit teacherturnedvirtualassistant.com/resources to access your free resources.

# CONCLUSION:

## Answering the Call

"Being confident of this, that He who began a good work in you will carry it on to completion until the day of Christ Jesus."

Philippians 7:6

Friend, the answer to figuring out your calling is no secret. God won't force you to follow His plan for you. He is a loving Father, and He has given you the gift of choice. The answer to being in true alignment with God's purpose for your life, to following His plan for you, is found in your YES.

Once you've made that decision to follow God

wherever He is leading you, no matter how scared you might be, you will notice the mountains that move out of your way. Our God is a mighty God, and He gives generously to those who love Him fully and follow Him faithfully. Once you choose to trust Him, there is nothing that you can't accomplish.

> *The difference between the called and the chosen is the chosen choose what God called them to, no matter where the choice takes them.*
> *—Hope D. Blackwell*

## MY PRAYER FOR YOU:

I pray that God would give you the tools and abilities you need to overcome any roadblock that you may face in your journey. You have everything you need inside of you to become who God has called you to be—all you have to do is go.

Start before you're ready.

Take that step of faith.

Seek support from fellow sons and daughters of Christ.

Know that I am here cheering you on.

Go where God has called you.

## NEXT STEPS:

Curious whether becoming a Virtual Assistant is the answer you've been praying for? I encourage you to check out my free workshop, "The Number 1 Way to Quit Teaching and Start Working from Home in 6 Months or Less." You can register for free at ariannavernier.com/free-workshop.

Feeling the call from God and ready to go all-in and pursue becoming a Virtual Assistant so you can work from home and spend more time with your babies? The Teacher Turned Virtual Assistant program is for you. You can learn more and grab your spot at teacherturnedvirtualassistant.com.

Teacher Turned...

# ACKNOWLEDGEMENTS:

I am blessed with an amazing support system that has pushed me to follow God's path for my life, even when I went kicking and screaming.

I'm thankful for my husband Reid for encouraging me and believing in me, even when I didn't necessarily believe in myself. I thank God every day for giving me you to share this life with.

Thank you to my kids, who are the biggest reason that I've chased these dreams God has placed on my heart. You give me the energy to keep going and help me find my why again whenever I'm lost.

Thank you to my mom, Pam, for always being a listening ear throughout this journey, for always answering my calls, and celebrating every small win with me. Thank you to my dad, for being the one I can always go to for advice and teaching me that I can do anything I set my mind Thank you to my family and friends, who cheer me on and pray for me daily. I couldn't have done this without you.

And most importantly, thank you to our sweet, loving, kind Father in Heaven, who called me here. I can't wait to see where You lead me next.

www.ingramcontent.com/pod-product-compliance
Lightning Source LLC
Chambersburg PA
CBHW070436130626
46553CB00006B/2221